# WOMEN WRITERS

## HIDDEN IN HISTORY

Petrice Custance

CRABTREE
Publishing Company
www.crabtreebooks.com

**Author:** Petrice Custance

**Editorial director:** Kathy Middleton

**Editors:** Sarah Eason, Ellen Rodger

**Proofreaders:** Jennifer Sanderson, Elizabeth DiEmanuele

**Design:** Paul Myerscough and Jessica Moon

**Cover design:** Emma DeBanks and Jessica Moon

**Illustrations:** Jessica Moon

**Photo research:** Rachel Blount

**Production coordinator and**
 **Prepress technician:** Margaret Amy Salter

**Print coordinator:** Katherine Berti

Written, developed, and produced by Calcium

**Photo Credits:**
t=Top, c=Center, b=Bottom, l= Left, r=Right

Inside: Library of Congress: p. 32; Jack Delano:
p. 31; Shutterstock: Everett Art: p. 12; Fizkes: p.
7; Kavon McKenzie: p. 43; Paralaxis: p. 39; Pi-
Lens: p. 36; Stocksnapper: p. 9b; De Visu: p. 27;
Oleg Znamenskiy: p. 45; Wikimedia Commons:
pp. 5, 25; Mary Astell: p. 10t; Daderot: pp. 19,
23; Jacques-Louis David: p. 16; G. Garitan: p.
17; Olympe de Gouges: p. 15t; Guinnog: p. 41;
Isidore Stanislas Helman after Charles Monnet: p.
13; Hiroshige: p. 20; Gabriël_Metsu: p. 10b; Emilia
Lanier: p. 9t; Library of Congress: p. 33; Marianne
Loir: p. 6; RKO: p. 29t; Maurice Quentin de
La Tour: p. 14; Henry Trotter: p. 42; Carl Van
Vechten, restored by Adam Cuerden: p. 34.

---

**Library and Archives Canada Cataloguing in Publication**

Title: Women writers : hidden in history / Petrice Custance.
Names: Custance, Petrice, author.
Description: Series statement: Hidden history |
 Includes bibliographical references and index.
Identifiers: Canadiana (print) 20200153307 |
 Canadiana (ebook) 20200153315 |
 ISBN 9780778773030 (hardcover) |
 ISBN 9780778773092 (softcover) |
 ISBN 9781427124807 (HTML)
Subjects: LCSH: Women authors—Biography—Juvenile literature.
 | LCSH: Women authors—History—Juvenile literature.
Classification: LCC PN471 .C87 2020 | DDC j809/.89287—dc23

**Library of Congress Cataloging-in-Publication Data**

Names: Custance, Petrice, author.
Title: Women writers hidden in history / Petrice Custance.
Description: New York, New York : Crabtree Publishing Company,
 [2020] | Series: Hidden history | Includes index.
Identifiers: LCCN 2019054375 (print) | LCCN 2019054376 (ebook)
 ISBN 9780778773030 (hardcover) |
 ISBN 9780778773092 (paperback) | ISBN 9781427124807 (ebook)
Subjects: LCSH: Women authors--Biography--Juvenile literature. |
 Women authors--History--Juvenile literature.
Classification: LCC PN471 .C87 2020 (print) | LCC PN471
 (ebook) | DDC 809/.89287--dc23
LC record available at https://lccn.loc.gov/2019054375
LC ebook record available at https://lccn.loc.gov/2019054376

---

# Crabtree Publishing Company

www.crabtreebooks.com    1-800-387-7650

Printed in the U.S.A./022020/CG20200102

**Published in Canada**
Crabtree Publishing
616 Welland Ave.
St. Catharines, Ontario
L2M 5V6

**Published in the United States**
Crabtree Publishing
PMB 59051
350 Fifth Avenue, 59th Floor
New York, New York 10118

**Published in the United Kingdom**
Crabtree Publishing
Maritime House
Basin Road North, Hove
BN41 1WR

**Published in Australia**
Crabtree Publishing
Unit 3 - 5 Currumbin Court
Capalaba
QLD 4157

# CONTENTS

# CHAPTER 1

# HISTORY'S HIDDEN HEROINES

Before the 20th century, most of the writers studied in classrooms were men. The message was loud and clear: men's writing was the writing worth studying and women's writing should be ignored. By the 1900s, things began to change and women writers finally began to get their due.

## Got the Message?

Entire generations of readers were finally introduced to a whole range of women writers. These include writers from distant history, such as Christine de Pizan, the awesome French **feminist** author from the 1300s. Aphra Behn, thought to be the first female **professional** author, is often studied, too. Many of these writers, such as Jane Austin and sister scribes Anne, Emily, and Charlotte Brontë, changed our views of women's lives. But these women writers have usually been studied separately from men, in a group of their own.

*The Brontë sisters, Anne (left), Emily (center), and Charlotte (right), wrote some of the most gripping novels of the 1800s .*

Colette was born on January 28, 1873, in Burgundy, France. She is shown here with her family. Some of her later novels were in part based on her childhood and teenage years in her village.

## Women, Are you Serious?

The idea that women's writing is less serious and therefore less valuable than men's writing is certainly not new and still exists. In 2013, Wikipedia editors began removing women authors from its American **Novelists** page and placing them on a separate page called American Women Novelists. This left the main American Novelists page featuring almost all men. After a huge outcry, Wikipedia added the women back to the main page.

## Hiding Who They Were

Throughout history, many women have attempted to avoid being labeled as a woman writer, in the hope of being taken more seriously. Some have chosen to write under the name Anonymous, which means unknown, and some wrote under a man's name. In the most famous example, Charlotte, Emily, and Anne Brontë published, or made public, their books under the names Currer, Ellis, and Acton Bell.

### HIDDEN HISTORY

### Hidden by her Husband

The French writer Collette began her writing hidden away from her readers, with her husband taking the glory for her work. Beginning in 1900, Colette wrote four novels in the Claudine series. All four books were published under her husband's name. They all became huge bestsellers. But, when Collette wanted to tell the world that she was the author, her husband refused. Collette decided enough was enough and divorced him. She then went on to become a world-famous writer.

5

## So, Why Are the Stories Hidden?

In a movie based on the writer Collette's life, there is a line that says, "The hand that holds the pen writes history." That line perfectly explains why women writers throughout the ages have been forgotten. Until the late 1900s, most of the hands holding the pens and writing the history books belonged to men. Education for most women was also very rare, so only a few were able to write at all.

When deciding which writers would be remembered across the centuries, most **historians** focused on the writing of men, and most often, white European men. This meant that the many women who had been writing throughout history were hardly spoken about. Their books went out of print and they were forgotten. Because people were mainly interested in men's writing, it helped strengthen the idea that writing is for men only. This left many centuries of women believing their voice was not important. We will never know how many women would have picked up a pen if they had believed their work and ideas had value.

*Gabrielle Émilie Le Tonnelier de Breteuil, Marquise du Châtelet, was a wealthy French writer who lived in the 1700s. She was unusual for her time because, unlike most other women writing, a number of her works were published.*

*By the 20th century, women writers such as Virginia Woolf were beginning to become more accepted in society. Virginia became one of the most famous women authors of her time.*

## Women No Longer Hidden

But there is good news! More and more people around the world are now tracking down the forgotten women writers of history. Projects such as The New Historia, Project Continua, and Project Vox are sharing the works and telling the stories of many incredible women.

## Searching for Hidden Heroines

Andrew Janiak, one of the people who began Project Vox, made an important discovery during the 1990s. He came across a **philosopher** named Emilie Du Chatelet. Janiak researched Du Chatelet and found that, in the 1730s and 1740s, she had written many important philosophical essays, letters, and books. Today, thanks to Janiak and Project Vox, Du Chatelet is being read and discussed in classrooms. And thanks to hard-working researchers around the world, more and more women writers are being rediscovered and taking their rightful places in the history books. Read on to discover some of the fascinating women writers the world should know about.

*With the use of modern technology, researchers are now able to easily share information about women writers with other researchers all over the world, helping to spread the word about these hidden heroines of history.*

# CHAPTER 2

# EPIC IN
# EUROPE

When you journey through European history, you travel through a world filled with wonderful writers. Let's take a trip into the past and learn about some of the awesome women writers who have helped make Europe epic!

## Aemilia Lanyer, the Real Shakespeare?

In 1973, an historian saved Aemilia Lanyer from being lost from history forever—but for the wrong reason. The historian believed that Aemilia was the "Dark Lady" mentioned in several of William Shakespeare's **sonnets**. Perhaps Shakespeare had been in love with her? Soon, other researchers tried to find out more about Aemilia. They discovered that, rather than being Shakespeare's love, she had actually been an important writer herself. In fact, she had been one of the first women in England to publish a book of poetry. That book was probably England's first feminist text. There are even now a few researchers who think Aemilia may have been the true author of William Shakespeare's works. So, who was this mysterious woman?

## Shaking Things Up

Aemilia Lanyer was born in 1569 in London, England. Her father was a royal musician, and Aemilia spent much time in the court of Queen Elizabeth I. In 1611, Aemilia published her book of poetry.

*Aemilia's poems were thought to be outrageous because they argued for women's freedom and equality.*

# SALVE DEVS
## REX IVDÆORVM.

*Containing,*

1 The Pafsion of Chrift.
2 Eues Apologie in defence of Women.
3 The Teares of the Daughters of Ierufalem.
4 The Salutation and Sorrow of the Virgine Marie.

With diuers other things not ynfit to be read.

Written by Miftris *Aemilia Lanyer*, Wife to Captaine *Alfonfo Lanyer* Seruant to the Kings Majeftie.

At LONDON
Printed by *Valentine Simmes* for *Richard Bonian*, and are to be fold at his Shop in Paules Churchyard, at the

## KEEPING GOOD COMPANY

From an early age, Aemilia was surrounded by women who encouraged her education. As a girl, she was neighbors with Anne Locke, the first English author of a sonnet sequence, or a group of sonnets linked together. After her father's death, Aemilia was educated in the home of Susan Bertie, Countess of Kent, who believed girls should receive the same education as boys. Aemilia then lived in the home of Lady Anne Clifford, who loved literature and was a respected writer herself.

*This is the title page of Aemilia's book of poems. At the bottom of the page, the text shows that the book was printed by Valentine Simmes. He was the finest printer in England and also printed plays by famous writers, such as Shakespeare. What does this tell us about the value of Aemilia's book?*

## Female Fan Club

Each poem in the book began with a special **dedication** to a woman Aemilia admired. It was very unusual at the time for women to speak highly of other women in this way. Aemilia's dedications show that she hoped one of the women would support her and perhaps give her money, so she could turn writing into a job. This seems to not have happened, and it's thought she never published again. Unless, of course, she published many works under the name William Shakespeare! There is no evidence, or proof, of this, and there is not even any evidence that Aemilia and Shakespeare ever met. However, several names in Shakespeare's works do seem to link to names of important people in Aemilia's life. But, whether there was any connection to Shakespeare or not does not matter. Aemilia Lanyer has finally entered the history books because of her own great work.

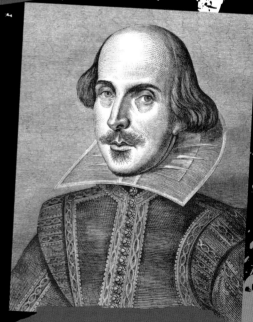

*Was William Shakespeare really a woman—Aemilia Lanyer?*

## Mary Astell, Feminist Free Spirit

How's this for a title: *A Serious Proposal to the Ladies for the Advancement of their True and Greatest Interest?* Published in 1694, this was the first book written by Mary Astell, England's first feminist thinker. Born in 1666, Mary is yet another woman writer who is only now getting into the history books. Though she was popular in her day, Mary was soon forgotten after her death.

## Life in London

Mary Astell was a lively and confident woman who found herself living alone in London in her 20s. In the late 1600s, this was very unusual for a woman. Mary was mostly self-taught and read everything she could. She wanted to be a writer, so she very quickly became friends with a group of literature-loving women who helped support her and get her published.

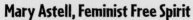

A Serious
PROPOSAL
TO THE
LADIES,
FOR THE
Advancement of their
True and Greatest
INTEREST.

PART I.

By a Lover of her SEX.

The Third Edition Corrected.

LONDON,
Printed by *T. W.* for *R. Wilkin,* at the *King's-Head* in St. *Paul's Church-Yard,* 1696.

Mary's respect for other women is made clear on the title page of her book, which is printed with the words "By a Lover of her Sex."

In the 1600s, the only women who could read and write usually came from wealthy families that could afford to educate them. Mary felt that all women should be given an education, no matter how rich or poor they were.

## Equal Minds

Mary believed women were just as smart as men, and that they deserved the same **right** as men to an education. She believed that education for women was, as the title of her first book suggested, in their true and greatest interest. In fact, she thought an educated mind was the key to achieving happiness and well-being. When some of the leading thinkers of the day spoke against her ideas about **gender** equality, she responded by asking, "If all men are born free, how is it that women are born slaves?"

## Just for Girls

Mary also thought it would be great for all women to be educated in girls-only schools, where they could live and learn together, similar to the schools that boys went to. In her later years, Mary managed to set up and run a school for girls only. Mary decided what the girls would be taught. All lessons were based on the idea of gender equality.

Mary wanted to make sure that her work was read by other people. She knew that to spread her words, they must be published.

## CLIMBING THE LADDER

When Mary arrived in London, she set about talking to the people who could help her begin her writing journey. She decided to send a few of her texts to the archbishop of Canterbury. He liked the look of Mary's work and set up an introduction with the publisher, who then printed her books.

## Olympe de Gouges, Fighting with the Pen

Olympe de Gouges would have loved Twitter! She was passionate about women's rights and against any type of inequality, including **slavery**. She was an author who wrote over 40 plays, 70 political essays, and two novels. All of her works were written to help bring about political change. But the leaders of the **French Revolution** decided Olympe had gone way too far and needed to be stopped. This would eventually lead to the execution of Olympe in 1793. Even today, Olympe is still being silenced by being denied her rightful place in the Pantheon, the building in which important French people are buried.

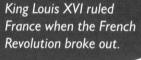

King Louis XVI ruled France when the French Revolution broke out.

## Rebel from the South

Olympe was born as Marie Gouze in 1748, in the south of France. From her earliest childhood, Olympe had a wild and free spirit. In 1770, Marie moved to Paris to become a writer. At this time, she gave herself a new name, Olympe de Gouges. This was an exciting time in which a lot of new ideas were talked about. It was called the Age of Enlightenment.

Olympe began going to meetings where human rights and equality were discussed. These ideas appealed to Olympe. She began writing anti-slavery plays. She hoped that they would help put an end to the slavery still taking place in the French-run countries abroad.

Olympe was angry at King Louis XVI for allowing slavery to continue, saying, "Men everywhere are equal… Kings who are **just** do not want slaves." Olympe faced threats of violence over her anti-slavery position, but she did not back down.

## Rebelling Against the Rich

In the 1700s, there was a lot of trouble in France. Unfair **taxation** and bad harvests had left many French people poor and hungry. There were also rumors that wealthy French people were storing food for themselves. Olympe wrote about this in newspapers and essays, sharing that the "heartless rich stash away their wealth."

On October 5, 1789, the women of Paris rose up in anger and marched to the Palace of Versailles. This was one of the earliest events of the French Revolution and eventually led to the arrest and execution of King Louis XVI. The Revolution had succeeded and France became a **republic**.

## FIGHTING FOR THE KING

After King Louis XVI was arrested, Olympe offered to be part of his legal defense team. Olympe argued that every person, even the king, deserved a fair trial. She was also against the death penalty, which is an order to kill a person. She argued that Louis should leave the country rather than be executed. But any sign of supporting the king was seen as acting against the Revolution. This likely led to Olympe's death sentence.

During the French Revolution, many wealthy people, known as nobles, were put to death. Most were killed by being **beheaded**, using a machine called a **guillotine**, shown below.

## The Birth of a Better World?

At first, Olympe was happy about the French Revolution. She believed she shared the same ideas as the leaders of the Revolution and that a better world was about to be born. *Declaration of the Rights of Man and of the Citizen*, the text that spoke about the aims of the Revolution, had been written in part based on the **philosophy** of Jean-Jacques Rousseau. The document talked about the idea of liberty (freedom), equality, and fraternity (brotherhood).

## Equality, but Just for Men

However, it soon became clear that when the *Declaration of the Rights of Man and of the Citizen* referred to equality, it meant equality for men, not women. The leaders of the Revolution had no interest in giving up their power. But Olympe hoped to persuade them that equality should be for everyone, including women. Cheered on by women supporters, Olympe wrote an essay called *Declaration of the Rights of Woman and the Female Citizen*.

## Right to Die, Right to Vote

One of Olympe's arguments was that if, like men, women could be executed, they also, like men, had the right to take part in politics. Olympe hoped her essay would encourage people to seriously think about the rights of women. But, this was never allowed. Instead, the Revolution leaders began cutting back the freedoms of French women even more. They could not meet in groups of more than four. Arguing against the leaders of the Revolution was also made against the law. The women of France had fewer rights than before the Revolution started!

Jean-Jaques Rousseau was an important writer of his time who changed many people's ideas about society.

## NOT A FAN OF WOMEN

Jean-Jacques Rousseau stood up for Enlightenment ideals. He wrote a lot about the importance of human rights and equality. But, he also wrote a lot about how men were better than women, such as, "Men should be active and strong, women passive and weak." So, not exactly a friend to women!

## I Will Not Give Up!

But, Olympe refused to give up. The leaders of the Revolution lost their way, but she still believed it was possible for the promising ideas of the Enlightenment to take hold in France. She published an essay entitled *The Three Urns*, in which she argued that one of three types of government would be the best way forward for France and all its people: a republic, a **federalist** government, or a **constitutional monarchy**. It was the mention of a constitutional monarchy, seen as a show of support for the king, that led to Olympe's arrest on July 20, 1793.

LES TROIS URNES,
OU LE SALUT DE LA PATRIE.
Par un VOYAGEUR AÉRIEN.

*This is the* The Three Urns *poster that was to be Olympe's downfall.*

*Many people believe that Olympe helped pave the way toward modern feminism, encouraging other women to find their voice and speak out.*

## You Will Die!

Olympe was charged with betraying the Revolution. She received a trial, but was refused a lawyer and had to speak for herself. After just one day of hearings, Olympe was sentenced to death by guillotine. The next day, on November 3, 1793, she was executed.

## Women, Know your Place!

Olympe's death was used as a warning to French women to never forget their proper place. After her death, women's rights were stripped away even more. In 1804, the French **emperor** Napoleon Bonaparte wrote and introduced the Napoleonic Code. This code was a series of laws that were terrible for women and denied them almost all rights. It was more than 150 years before the women of France finally began to gain some of the **political** equality that Olympe wanted.

## Wiped from the History Pages

After her death, Olympe was removed from history. Her papers were burned and only a few of her early texts remain. If she was mentioned in a history book, it was usually in a disrespectful way. Jules Michelet, a French historian, wrote about Olympe, "She allowed herself to act and write about more than one affair that her weak head did not understand."

*Napoleon Bonaparte believed that a woman's place was at home, caring for the family and keeping the house. He did not believe women should have rights equal to men.*

## Remembering a Heroine

As with so many forgotten women in history, it was the feminist movement (when women fought for equality) of the 1970s that led to Olympe becoming famous once more. Thanks to researchers, Olympe is beginning to receive the respect she deserves. The movement to have Olympe admitted to the Pantheon has so far failed.

Today, with so much talk about human rights, it is easy to imagine Olympe de Gouges tweeting and blogging away, working toward her hopes for equality for women that still have not fully been achieved.

In 2014, a statue of Olympe was displayed in France's **National Assembly** as a sign of respect and to remember one of France's great heroines.

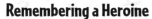

## HIDDEN HISTORY

### Words as Weapons

Olympe had a basic education and very little writing skills when she arrived in Paris. She did not even speak French at the time, but rather a language spoken often in the South of France, called Occitan. Olympe taught herself to write. This is quite amazing when you consider her words became powerful enough to make the men who had captured a king so frightened that they killed her.

Although Olympe was put to death by the guillotine, her words have lived on and inspire many other women around the world today.

# CHAPTER 3

## AWESOME IN ASIA

For centuries, Asia has been famous for its wonderful writing. But all the fame and glory went to men, and not women. Today, all of that is changing and Asia's wondrous women writers are finally in the spotlight.

### Enheduanna, the Poet Priestess

The history books have long shown men as the masters of written language. So it's not surprising that most people are shocked to discover the world's first known author was a woman. Some have even called her the **inventor** of literature itself! Her name was Enheduanna.

### People Persuader

Born in 2285 BCE, Enheduanna lived in Sumer, now southern Iraq, one of the world's first **civilizations**. She was the daughter of Sargon the Great, a king who controlled many areas, creating the world's first **empire**. Enheduanna was made a high **priestess** by her father. Her role was to bring together cities defeated by her father, so they would have just one ruler—her dad. One way she did this was by writing poems and **hymns** that spoke about the greatness of her father.

*Enheduanna wrote her poems and hymns on wet clay tablets with a reed for a pen.*

Early in the Sumerian civilization, under law, women were equal to men. They were educated and held positions of power. That changed when Enheduanna's father seized control. He immediately began taking freedom away from women and giving all power to men. As a high priestess and a princess, Enheduanna was able to keep her freedom and power. This allowed her to have the voice that her father would not allow other women.

## Making It Personal

In the 1920s, **archaeologists** discovered tablets with six poems and 42 hymns written by Enheduanna. Not only was it amazing that a woman had written so many works within Sumerian civilization, but she had also signed them! Enheduanna was the first known person in history to sign her work. And she was the first writer in history to write about herself. One of the poems was called *Lady of the Largest Heart*, and was written in praise of the **goddess** Inanna. In it, Enheduanna discusses events of her life, as well as her feelings, hopes, and fears. Enheduanna begins the poem by boldly declaring "I am Enheduanna."

There must be so many women in history who wanted to write, but had been told it was not for women—imagine if they had known about Enheduanna! Perhaps their histories would have been quite different…

*This is the clay tablet on which Enheduanna wrote her poem,* Lady of the Largest Heart. *When **translated**, it reads:* As I, Inanna, approached the mountain it showed me no respect, as I approached the mountain range of Ebih it showed me no respect. Since they showed me no respect, since they did not put their noses to the ground for me, since they did not rub their lips in the dust for me, I shall personally fill the soaring mountain range with my terror. Against its magnificent sides I shall place magnificent battering rams…

## Murasaki Shikibu, the World's First Novelist

Historians have long-claimed that *Don Quixote*, written by Miguel de Cervantes in 1605, was the world's first novel. But today, many believe that the world's first novelist was actually a woman! There is only one problem—we do not know her real name.

## The Hidden Heroine

The author known as Murasaki Shikibu was born around 973 CE in Japan, into a rich and powerful family. We know some details of her life because her diary survives. She is called Murasaki, because that is the name of the heroine in her novel, *The Tale of Genji*. Shikibu comes from the name of her father's government position. In the 900s in Japan, many women were known by their father's or their husband's name. This is likely why historians have never come across her real name.

## Loving to Learn

Murasaki was curious and loved to learn. Her father helped her with her studies, which was very unusual for Japanese women in the 900s. In her diary, Murasaki says because she was so intelligent, her father wished she had been born a boy. In 998 she married, but her husband died just a few years later. It was after he died that Murasaki likely began writing her novel.

*This illustration is from a book of* The Tale of Genji. *It shows a nobleman and a noblewoman at the Japanese court.*

## MILLENNIAL MURASAKI

In 2008, Japan celebrated the 1,000th **anniversary** of *The Tale of Genji*. The festivities included a robot version of Murasaki that could speak passages from the novel.

### Writing with Feeling

*The Tale of Genji* tells the story of an emperor's son who treats those around him cruelly. It is more than 1,000 pages long and blends **fiction** with poetry. It was very unusual for its time because much of the book talks about the deep feelings and thoughts of its characters. The novel also describes life at the **imperial court** with such careful detail that historians have used it to learn much about this period in Japan.

### Loved by the Ladies

Murasaki was a **lady-in-waiting** to the empress during the time she wrote the novel. She shared chapters of her novel with others at court. The novel was loved by the women at court. Diaries written by them describe their excitement at reading *The Tale of Genji*. The novel was made into many handwritten copies, which were read throughout Japan.

*As well as writing* **The Tale of the Genji,** *Murasaki also kept a diary while she was at court. In it, she wrote what she saw and thought about living among the royal family and also wrote about her feelings of loneliness after her husband's death.*

## The Women of Jiangyong County, Stories of Sisterhood

Sometime in the 1960s in China, an elderly woman fainted in a train station. When the Chinese police went through her belongings to find out who she was, they found items with strange markings on them. Believing her to be a spy, the police arrested her. However, the lady was not a spy. The markings on the items in her bag were actually Nushu—the world's only secret language just for women!

## Women Only

Nushu means women's writing. It was created by the women of Jiangyong county, in the Hunan **province** of southern China, so that they could share thoughts and feelings with each other. Nushu often included messages, riddles (word puzzles), and songs. No one is exactly sure when Nushu began. Some think it goes as far back as 1,000 years, but most historians believe it was developed in the 1800s. Nushu is based on Chinese **characters**, but its lines are longer and thinner. Women would write the language in letters, on objects such as paper fans, or sew it into fabrics, such as quilts and handkerchiefs. Nushu existed only in Jiangyong, a hard-to-reach place in the mountains, and this is likely why it never spread outside of the area.

*Reading Nushu was a lifeline for young Chinese girls, who had had their feet bound (see next page). It helped them keep in contact with other girls when it was impossible to travel to meet them.*

The feet of Chinese women were so tightly bound (see below) that they could fit into shoes as pointed and narrow as these.

## Freedom and Fun

Nushu was passed down from mother to daughter. The women usually had not been educated, so most were unable to read or write. Nushu gave them the means to share their thoughts on paper. This secret language was important to Chinese women because, before modern times, they led difficult lives. Poor women worked hard all day and wealthier women spent much of their time indoors, rarely seeing other people. Also at this time in China, mainly in wealthier families, many young girls and women had their feet bound. This was a **cultural** practice in which delicate, small feet were thought to be beautiful. But foot binding was painful and kept the girls from walking easily. To bind the feet, the bones were broken, then the feet were tightly wrapped to keep them from growing. When the girls became adults, their feet were so small that could walk only in tiny steps. Nushu helped the girls and women forget about their pain.

## FROM THE HEART

In 2004, Yang Huanyi passed away. She was one of the last women who could read and write Nushu. In 2002, Yang told a reporter why Nushu was so special to her. "When I learned Nushu, it was meant to exchange (share) our thoughts and letters with friends and sisters. We wrote what was in our hearts and our true feelings."

Nushu helped create a special bond between sworn sisters. Sworn sisters were girls who grew up in the same village and became friends forever. No matter where life took them, they swore to always be friends. Nushu helped them keep talking to each other and keep their friendship.

## Stories from Sadness

When a woman in Hunan province married, it often meant leaving her village to join her new husband. On the third day after her wedding, she was given a special cloth-bound book. Written in Nushu by the bride's mother, sisters, aunts, cousins, grandmothers, and also sworn sisters, it included messages of hope and best wishes, as well as sadness at her leaving. The last pages of the book were left blank for the bride to use as a diary, written in Nushu.

The sworn sisters of Nushu were bound together forever by their shared thoughts and feelings.

24

*Life in ancient China could be very dull for many women, involving boring daily chores. Having a secret language like Nushu must have been exciting!*

## Buried with the Past

There are not many early Nushu works still in existence. One reason is that, during China's **Cultural Revolution**, which lasted from 1966 to 1976, Nushu was declared a "witches' script" and was banned. Many works of Nushu were destroyed during that time. Another reason so few works survive is that, when a woman died, her Nushu works were often buried with her or burned. This was so the woman's Nushu works could follow her into the afterlife, or life after death.

## Hidden No Longer

Today, Nushu is no longer a secret. People are working hard to keep the language alive. Dictionaries and texts in Nushu have been published. Nushu is no longer known by women only. Chinese women now go to school and university, so they are not cut off from the world as they once were. Foot binding is also now against the law. All of this means Nushu no longer needs to be only for women. After all, from the very beginning, Nushu was meant to be shared.

## Tarabai Shinde, Fighting for Women

Thanks to Google, many people are finally learning about Tarabai Shinde. The Indian feminist author has been included in Google's arts and culture section in a program called *Women in India: Unheard Stories*, which brings to light women who have had a big effect on India's culture.

## As Good as Any Man

Tarabai Shinde was a feminist **pioneer**. Her first and only published work, *A Comparison Between Women and Men*, is thought to be India's first feminist text. Published in 1882, Tarabai's writing caused as much of a stir then as it does today—because her work openly questioned religious teachings and texts that said men were better than women. Tarabai argued that men were not better than women. She demanded that women should be seen and treated as equals.

Along with her writing, Tarabai was famous for her confident personality. She was passionate about equality and the idea that all people should have the same chance to live a good life.

### It's Not Fair

Tarabai also wrote against the unfairness of the caste system. In Indian society, the caste system divides people into social levels. People are born into these levels and they are very difficult to change. What caste a person is in determines what job they can have, where they can live, and whom they can marry. This often creates great hardships for people.

### Trailblazing Tarabai

More than 100 years after Tarabai, the equality she argued for still has not been achieved. However, today, many young Indian women are finally discovering Tarabai's writing and feeling inspired by this determined woman.

## BULLIED INTO SILENCE

Following the publication of *A Comparison Between Women and Men*, Tarabai faced threats from people who were angry about her words. As a result, she never published again. The anger over her one great work is likely what caused her to fade from history.

*Tarabai knew that many women in India led difficult lives and did not have the same opportunities as men. She worked hard to try to change that.*

# CHAPTER 4

# AMAZING IN THE
# AMERICAS

The Americas have been home to famous writers who have wowed the world with their tales. Let us meet some of the unstoppable women who had so many awesome stories to tell.

**STRONGHEART**

## Hollywood Heroines

There is much talk today about the lack of women writers in Hollywood. In 2018, for the 100 top-grossing, or money-making, movies of the year, only 15 percent of the writers were women. But, it was not always this way. At the birth of Hollywood, beginning in the late 1890s, women wrote nearly 50 percent of all movies. In fact, women were incredibly active in all moviemaking roles.

## What Happened to the Women?

What happened? Why did women disappear from their roles behind the camera? It all boils down to money. In the late 1920s, Hollywood began to make the switch from silent to sound films. This required expensive equipment, so movie studios depended on large **loans** from banks. These banks began to demand that the studios be run like companies outside of movie-making, which meant putting men in charge. That meant the time of women as powerful forces behind the camera was over. Worse still, most of these women were left out of the history books.

*Jane Murfin has been called the busiest yet least-known **screenwriter** of early Hollywood. She wrote several movies, four of them starring her own dog, Strongheart, who became the world's first dog star. Strongheart has a star on the Hollywood Walk of Fame. Jane Murfin, the Academy Award nominated screenwriter, does not!*

The full story of women in early Hollywood is only just now coming to light. Here are just a few of the forgotten women writers of Hollywood:

Jeanie MacPherson was the lead screenwriter for Cecil B. DeMille, one of the first great directors in Hollywood. From 1915 to 1930 she wrote most of his major movies, including *The Ten Commandments*. However, in a 1957 interview, DeMille ruined her publically by saying, "She was not a good writer." After that, no one spoke about her or wrote about her in movie history. Only now are researchers trying to write her inspiring story again in the history pages.

Adela Rogers St. Johns was a **journalist**, novelist, and screenwriter. She wrote the original script for a 1932 movie called *What Price Hollywood?*

*What Price Hollywood?* was a hit in the 1930s. Four famous versions of St. Johns' story have been made, including the 2018 hit *A Star Is Born*, starring Lady Gaga.

HIDDEN HISTORY

### Silenced by Fear

The first feature-length Hollywood movie, released in 1915, was *The Birth of a Nation*. At the time, people thought its filming techniques were amazing. But, the movie was also horribly **racist** in the way it showed African Americans. Some people even think the movie encouraged the **Ku Klux Klan** to become active again. Drusilla Dunjee Houston, an African-American writer from Oklahoma, wrote a screenplay to fight back against the racism of *The Birth of a Nation*. Titled *Spirit of the Old South: The Maddened Mob*, the movie was never made because the Ku Klux Klan were active again in Oklahoma. Drusilla feared for her family's safety.

*The Ku Klux Klan is a violent group that targets African Americans. It began in 1865. Its members historically wore white clothing, including a peaked white hat.*

## Alice Dunbar-Nelson, Political Power Player

Many of Alice Dunbar-Nelson's most powerful and important stories were never published during her lifetime. Publishers in the early 1900s believed the American public would not want to read books that spoke about racism and inequality. For example, *The Stones of the Village* is the story of a mixed-race man named Victor who is of both African-American and white heritage, but is able to pass as white. The story focuses on the feelings and guilt that Victor feels when experiencing the freedoms and privileges that come with passing as white while other African Americans are experiencing racism. Such difficult feelings were something Alice knew much about.

*Alice loved to read books as a child and kept her love of reading all her life. She wanted to share her love of stories with the whole world through her writing.*

## Caught in the Middle

Alice Dunbar-Nelson was born in New Orleans in 1875. She was one of the first African Americans to be born free after the end of slavery. Alice was mixed race. Her mother was African American and her father was white. Alice saw herself as African American, but was sometimes mistaken for white. In **segregated** Louisiana, this sometimes allowed her to enter places, such as museums, that other African Americans could not. Alice was a gifted student and entered university at age 15. By the age of 17, Alice was working as a teacher. Alice would continue to teach off and on throughout her life.

This photograph shows an African-American man waiting for a coach in an area of the platform assigned to black people. They were kept separate from white people both on the platform and in the train itself.

## A Terrible Crime

Throughout her life, Alice worked to bring about racial justice. She pushed the passing of anti-lynching laws. Lynching is when a person accused of an offense is not allowed a legal trial and instead is murdered by a group of people. Lynching was a horrific problem in the southern United States. Many African Americans were murdered by white people. The anti-lynching laws Alice worked for were never passed and, amazingly, an anti-lynching law was not passed in the United States until 2018.

## HIDDEN HISTORY

### Stories of Hurt

In her essay *Brass Ankles Speaks*, Alice discussed a difficult reality of her life. Some darker-skinned African Americans were jealous of her lighter skin and treated her cruelly. She writes about wanting to be fully part of her African-American community and the pain of not being accepted. This is something that is rarely written because many African Americans find it hard to acknowledge and speak about it.

## Letters and Love

At age 20, Alice published her first book of short stories and poetry, *Violets and Other Tales*. Right from the start, her work spoke about gender and racial equality. Alice's book attracted the attention of the well-known African-American writer Paul Laurence Dunbar. They began writing letters to each other and, in 1898, they married. In the African-American community, they were thought of as a power couple, perhaps a little like the Beyoncé and Jay-Z of their day. However, the marriage was not a happy one and the couple separated.

## More than Just a Wife

Alice went on to marry two more times, but her first marriage continued to affect how she was seen as a writer. It was also likely the reason she was forgotten so quickly. Some historians preferred to view Alice as the wife of an important writer instead of a successful writer in her own right. Today, researchers and historians are finally giving her works the study and attention they deserve.

*Paul Laurence Dunbar was born on June 27, 1872. His mother and father were both slaves, who were then later freed. Paul wrote about what it was like to live in the southern United States as an African American.*

## Too Dirty for Women?

In between teaching and writing, Alice became involved in politics. In 1915, she joined the fight for women to get the vote. Alice came up against people from both races who did not want women to vote. Some white people didn't want women to get the vote because they worried white women wouldn't turn up to vote, but black women would, and so white people would be outvoted. Some black people didn't want women to get the vote because, due to racist laws called Jim Crow laws, many black women wouldn't be able to vote anyway. In this case, since white women would be able to, they would help outvote black people. When anyone said they thought politics was too dirty for women, Alice responded, "Politics is the only dirt we don't get into at present."

## GETTING NOWHERE?

Alice began keeping a diary at age 46. One of the first things she wrote was, "I lay in bed this morning thinking, forty-six years old and nowhere yet." Perhaps she felt that way because so much of her work remained unpublished at that time, because it spoke about race and inequality. It may not have seemed like it to her at the time, but Alice had already achieved something meaningful. Today, her work is read as powerful lessons about racism and inequality.

*These women are campaigning for women's rights. Alice was part of this movement that fought for the rights of women in the United States.*

WE DEMAND AN AMENDMENT TO THE UNITED STATES CONSTITUTION ENFRANCHISING WOMEN

WELCOME SUFFRAGE ENVOYS

## Hope in Harlem

The Harlem Renaissance was a time of hope and pride for African Americans. It occurred mostly throughout the 1920s, when artistic talent in the African-American community, particularly in Harlem in New York City, came to light. During the Harlem Renaissance, some of the greatest works of literature, music, and visual art the world has ever known were created.

## Finding out about Alice

Alice was part of this exciting movement. She was a source of inspiration to many of its writers. She also published some stories and essays in many of its publications and she wrote about the work of many of its great writers. However, much of Alice's fiction and poetry remained unpublished during her lifetime. This made it difficult for researchers to find her work and it is likely why her memory largely faded away. But, all of that is changing now. Much of Alice's writing has now been found and published and researchers are shining a light on her amazing work.

Bessie Smith was another woman who set the Harlem scene alight in the 1920s. She was an African-American Blues singer who became nicknamed the Empress of the Blues, because she was the most popular Blues singer of the time.

# OTHER HARLEM HEROINES

Most of the focus of the Harlem Renaissance has been on the men. But, work is now being done to discover more women members who have been hidden away in history. Jessie Redmon Fauset likely wrote the first novel of the Harlem Renaissance, called *There Is Confusion*. Ariel Williams Holloway wanted to be a concert pianist but, because she was African American, there weren't many opportunities. So, she began writing poetry and one of them, *Northboun*, is considered one of the best poems of the movement.

Nella Larsen was a nurse and librarian before writing two of what are now considered the greatest novels of the movement—Quicksand and Passing. She then left Harlem and writing behind and returned to nursing.

## Angela Sidney, Sharing Ancient Stories

Sometimes, words can be lost not because they have been written out of history on purpose, but because they are not being used or have not been written down. Many societies have handed down their culture and stories by speaking about them, instead of writing them. As a child, Angela Sidney loved to listen to her family tell stories about the history of the **Tagish peoples** of Canada's Yukon. As she grew older, Angela realized there were fewer and fewer people sharing Tagish stories and speaking the Tagish language. One day, she realized she was one of the last people who could speak Tagish well.

## Saving her History

Angela Sidney was born in 1902 in the Yukon. In the 1970s, as a Tagish Elder of the Delsheetaan Nation, she decided it was her responsibility to help keep the language, history, and culture of her people alive for future generations. She began writing books in Tagish, for both adults and children.

## A Storytelling Journey

Angela started making the long journey of more than 2,500 miles (4,000 km) from the Yukon to Toronto every year to share her stories with a wider audience. Local Yukon people decided to organize a storytelling festival to save her the long trip. From 1988 to 2008, the Yukon International Storytelling Festival was held in Whitehorse every year. Storytellers from around the world took part in the festival and shared their spoken stories.

*Whitehorse is one of the best places in the world to see the Aurora Borealis, or northern lights. It is a magical place to hold a storytelling festival.*

Angela was passionate about keeping the Tagish storytelling tradition alive and loved to share stories with young Tagish children.

### Rewarded for her Work

In 1986, Angela Sidney became the first **Indigenous** person from the Yukon to receive the Order of Canada, the second highest honor in the country. She was given the award because of her incredible work in keeping her people's stories and history alive.

## PASSING ON HER PASSION

Angela once said, "I have no money to leave for my grandchildren. My stories are my wealth." She passed away in 1991, safe in the knowledge that she had passed on the most precious thing she had to her grandchildren—her stories.

## Carolina Maria de Jesus, Writing for the Poor

There had never been anything like it before! A diary, never written to be published, that told a story about living in extreme poverty, or in very poor conditions, in a slum, known as a favela, in São Paulo, Brazil. The diary belonged to Carolina Maria de Jesus, a black woman born in 1914. When her diary was discovered by a journalist in 1958, Carolina was a single mother selling scrap paper and cans to support herself and her three children. Every night, to keep her mind off of her hunger and fear, she wrote in her diary about daily life in the favela.

## A Hungry Heroine

Carolina's descriptions of poverty and hunger were simple and devastating. She wrote about the pain she felt when her hungry children asked for more food but there was none. She also wrote about politics: "Brazil needs to be led by a person who has known hunger. Hunger is also a teacher. Who has gone hungry learns to think of the future and of the children."

Carolina's diary was filled with stories about the difficult lives of people in the favelas. It showed people the truth about life in the slums—a truth that had been hidden from the world until Carolina wrote about it.

## Sensational Storyteller

Carolina's diary was published in 1960. It was an instant hit and quickly became a bestseller around the world. At that time, no one had ever written about life in a favela so honestly. Carolina was suddenly thrown into the spotlight and she was not prepared for it. Her favela neighbors were cruel to her because she had written about them. She also hated press and the lack of privacy that came with her fame. Some people in Brazil even doubted she had really written the diary.

## Cheated and Forgotten

Carolina published some other works, but they did not sell well. It was also said that her publishing company cheated her out of some of the money from the international sales. Carolina was soon forgotten. Although it was a sad end to the story, the power of Carolina's words shone a light on and gave a voice to some of the world's poorest people.

### AGAINST ALL ODDS

When Carolina's diary was published in Brazil, it sold 10,000 copies in three days. It went on to sell in more than 40 countries and it was translated into 13 languages.

*It is estimated that 6 percent of Brazil's population live in favelas. In São Paulo today, there are about 1,600 favelas.*

# CHAPTER 5

# ACING IT IN AFRICA

Africa is a vibrant, exciting continent—and the stories of its women writers are just as thrilling and inspiring.

## Noni Jabavu, a Heroine at Last

If you do an Internet search for "Noni Jabavu," you will find blog posts written by young African women discussing how thrilled they are to have found her writings. Noni was the first black South African woman to publish an **autobiography**. But, she has not been widely known in her home country until recent years.

## Educated Out of Country

Born in 1919, in the Eastern Cape in South Africa, Noni came from a comfortable and well-educated family. At age 13, Noni's parents sent her to England for her education. Noni told the story of first meeting her English **guardians** in a home called Tsalta. The name of the home spelled backward was "At last."

*Noni made engine parts for army vehicles in England during World War II (1939 to 1945). It was a world away from writing!*

## Wartime Working

Noni's family wanted her to become a doctor, but that did not interest her. She studied music, and then trained to work in film until World War II broke out.

## Writing in Dangerous Times

After the war, still in London, Noni found her calling. She began writing. But, just as her new job was beginning, the situation drastically changed in South Africa. In 1948, the country separated its people based on race. The white people, who were the smallest group in the country, ran the government, made all the laws, and treated the nonwhite people, who were the largest group in the country, badly. This system of racism was called apartheid, which meant "apartness."

## Love Is a Crime

One of the country's laws was that people from different races were not allowed to marry. This law would greatly affect Noni's life. In 1951, while still in England, she married a white man. In her home country, under apartheid law, their marriage was a crime. Noni was now considered a criminal in her country! If she visited South Africa, she could be arrested if seen with her husband.

### YOU CAN'T TELL STORIES!

In 1975, Miriam Tlali was the first black South African woman to publish a novel. The book, *Muriel at Metropolitan*, was immediately banned by the Censorship Board, the writing **watchdog** for South Africa. Her second novel, *Amandla*, was published in 1980. It was also immediately banned. Both books were unbanned in 1986.

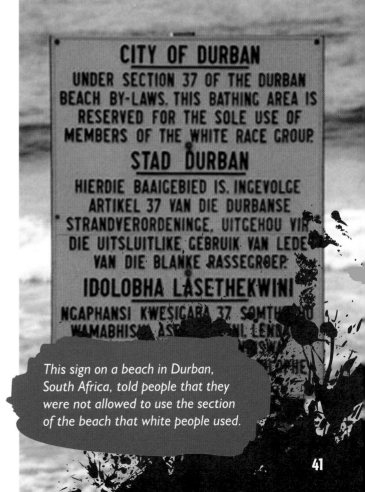

This sign on a beach in Durban, South Africa, told people that they were not allowed to use the section of the beach that white people used.

## Torn Between Two Worlds

Noni wrote about her pride in being South African and her love of her country's traditions, but also of the trouble that white rule had brought. She wrote too about feeling torn between two worlds, black South Africa and white England, where she was educated and from where her husband came. She wrote about not really fitting into either world. This struggle was explored in her two autobiographies, *Drawn in Colour*, published in 1960, and *The Ochre People*, published in 1963. Noni wrote, "I belong to two worlds with two loyalties: South Africa, where I was born, and England, where I was educated."

Noni's travels opened her eyes to how little white people understood black cultures and helped inspire her writing.

Apartheid ended in South Africa in 1994. South Africans are now forging brighter futures for themselves, but the legacies of oppression take time to overcome.

Noni's travels took her to Jamaica, where she spoke about the island's beauty.

## Writing All Over the World

In 1961, Noni became the first African and the first woman editor of the British publication *The New Strand*. She also continued writing for different international publications, often talking about apartheid in South Africa. Noni also traveled all over the world. At different times, she lived in Jamaica, Kenya, Uganda, and Zimbabwe.

## Her Story Ends

Noni died in 2008. She had dreamed of passing away in her beloved South Africa and her wish was granted. Noni's family is working hard to make sure that her work is not forgotten. Today, many young South Africans are now learning about Noni and her important contributions to their country's literature.

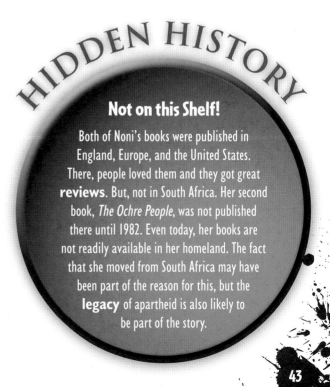

## HIDDEN HISTORY

### Not on this Shelf!

Both of Noni's books were published in England, Europe, and the United States. There, people loved them and they got great **reviews**. But, not in South Africa. Her second book, *The Ochre People*, was not published there until 1982. Even today, her books are not readily available in her homeland. The fact that she moved from South Africa may have been part of the reason for this, but the **legacy** of apartheid is also likely to be part of the story.

### Neshani Andreas, the Lonely Writer

Neshani Andreas was born in Namibia in southwest Africa in 1964. She was a shy child who dreamed of writing, but her family did not support her dream. She trained and worked as a teacher, but always longed to write. One day, she mentioned to a friend that she hoped to be a writer one day. Her friend asked if he could read some of her writing. She gave him some pages and he thought they were great. Neshani said, "This was one of the most treasured moments in my life. I had met the first person in my life who showed interest and understanding in my writing."

*Neshani loved writing about real life and experiences and would lose herself in her world of words as she wrote.*

## What it Means to be a Woman

Her friend's words gave Neshani the encouragement she needed. The words flowed from her pen. The result was *The Purple Violet of Oshaantu*. The novel is about women's friendship and it explores how women are seen in Namibian society. It describes daily life for women in the countryside of Namibia in a completely honest way. It explores both the good and bad parts of the communities there and it includes scenes of **domestic violence**. After its release, the novel got great reviews, both in Namibia and around the world.

## Hiding from the Truth

Many Namibians did not like how their country was shown in the novel, particularly the talk about domestic violence. Some Namibians felt let down by Neshani. Some even began to suggest that she had not written the novel herself. Neshani died of lung cancer in 2011. At the time of her death, she had just completed her second manuscript. It has not been published yet.

*Neshani wrote about ordinary life for rural Namibian women and shared how they spent their days.*

# GLOSSARY

**anniversary** The marking of an event a year or more after it happened

**archaeologists** People who examine buildings and objects left behind by people in the past to find out more about them

**autobiography** The story of a person's life written by the person it is about

**beheaded** Had their head cut off

**characters** Symbols that have meanings, such as letters

**civilizations** Organized groups of people

**constitutional monarchy** A form of monarchy in which a sovereign's authority is written in a constitution

**cultural** Related to a people with the same arts, language, and religious beliefs

**Cultural Revolution** A movement in the People's Republic of China, lasting from 1966 to 1976

**dedication** Words in praise of someone, or to acknowledge someone at the start of a book, for example

**domestic violence** Violent or aggressive behavior within a home

**emperor** A man who rules an empire

**empire** A large area of land, often containing many countries, ruled over by one person

**federalist** A system in which many states, or areas, of one country are controlled by one organization

**feminist** A person who believes in the equality of the sexes

**fiction** Writing that is not factual, such as a novel or short story

**French Revolution** An uprising against the monarchy in France, lasting from 1789 to 1799

**gender** How a person identifies, such as male or female

**goddess** A female higher power that is worshiped by people

**guardians** People who care for a young person, but who are not their parents

**guillotine** A machine used to behead people, or cut their heads from their bodies

**historians** People who record history

**hymns** Religious songs

**imperial court** The court of an empire

**Indigenous** The first people who lived in an area

**inventor** A person who comes up with the idea for something, or is the first person to do something

**journalist** A person who records the news

**just** Right or fair

**Ku Klux Klan** An American group who believes white people are better than black people

**lady-in-waiting** A woman who helped important women in royal courts

**legacy** Something that a person, event, or system is remembered for once dead or ended

**loans** Money lent by banks and other similar organizations, or money lent from one person to another

**National Assembly** The elected legislature, or government, in France

**novelists** People who write stories

**philosopher** A person who studies knowledge and thought

**philosophy** The study of knowledge and thought

**pioneer** The first person to do something

**political** Related to politics

**priestess** A woman who has religious power

**professional** A person who is paid to do a specific job

**province** An area within a country, which often has its own local laws

**racist** The judgment of someone based upon their race

**republic** A state in which power is held by the people and their elected representatives

**reviews** Comments about a movie, piece of art, piece of music, or other artistic work

**right** A protection that people have

**screenwriter** A person who writes the story and dialogue, or spoken words, for a movie

**segregated** Set apart from each other, based on racial or religious lines

**slavery** A condition in which someone is held against their will and forced to work for another person

**sonnets** Poems made up of 14 lines

**Tagish peoples** An Indigenous people who lived in Yukon, Canada

**taxation** A form of taking money from people by the government or king or queen to pay for things, such as public transportation and public buildings

**translated** Changed into another language

**watchdog** An organization that closely watches what people are doing in a certain area, for example, movie-making or writing

## LEARNING MORE

Read more about women who broke the rules and changed the world!

### Books
Ball, Heather. *Remarkable Women Writers*. Second Story Press, 2006.

Hazell, Rebecca. *Women Writers* (Women in the Arts). Abbeville Press, 2002.

Pankhurst, Kate. *Fantastically Great Women Who Changed the World*. Bloomsbury USA, 2016.

Reef, Catherine. *The Brontë Sisters: The Brief Lives of Charlotte, Emily, and Anne*. Clarion Books, 2015.

### Websites
Learn more about Nushu and its historical importance:
**https://en.unesco.org/courier/2018-1/nushu-tears-sunshine**

Discover some more great women writers and their wonderful books:
**https://bit.ly/2FpS9Hj**

Visit this site to sign up for the NaNoWriMo 30-day novel writing challenge. You can either sign up on your own or ask your teacher to enter your class:
**https://ywp.nanowrimo.org**

Visit this site to explore a digital database of incredible women and their important contributions to history:
**https://womenshistory.si.edu**

# INDEX

## ABOUT THE AUTHOR

Petrice Custance has written books on many fascinating topics, but discovering and writing about the amazing women writers who have been hidden in history has been one of her most exciting projects ever! Through this book, Petrice hopes to inspire other young women to pick up the pen and start writing their own stories.

48